Diggers

Aaron Frisch

CREATIVE EDUCATION

seedlings

Published by Creative Education
P.O. Box 227, Mankato, Minnesota 56002
Creative Education is an imprint of
The Creative Company
www.thecreativecompany.us

Design by Ellen Huber
Production by Chelsey Luther
Art direction by Rita Marshall
Printed in the United States of America

Photographs by Dreamstime (Anthonyata, Artzzz, Matthew
Heinrichs, Ying Feng Johansson, Witthayap), Getty Images
(Richard du Toit, kryczka), iStockphoto (Mark Atkins,
Eduardo Luatti Buyé, Mike Clarke, pic4you, vasilypetkov),
Shutterstock (Anteromite, Dmitry Kalinovsky, rodho, Milos
Stojanovic), SuperStock (Cultura Limited)

Library of Congress Cataloging-in-Publication Data
Frisch, Aaron.
Diggers / Aaron Frisch.
p. cm. — (Seedlings)
Summary: A kindergarten-level introduction to diggers,
covering their size, movement, role in the process of
construction, and such defining features as their arms
and buckets.
Includes bibliographical references and index.
ISBN 978-1-60818-340-1
1. Buckets (Excavating machinery)—Juvenile literature.
I. Title.

TA725.F753 2013
621.8'65—dc23   2012023420

First Edition
9 8 7 6 5 4 3 2 1

TABLE OF CONTENTS

Time to dig!

Diggers are big machines.

They make holes in the ground.

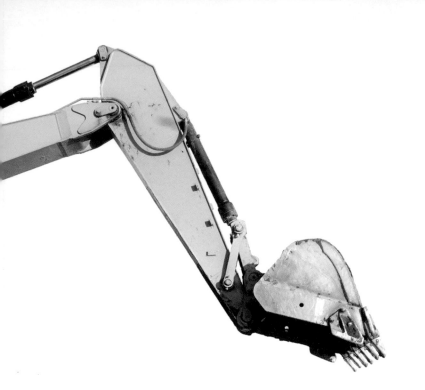

A digger has a strong arm. A big bucket is on the end of the arm.

A digger picks up dirt and rocks with its bucket. It puts the dirt and rocks in a dump truck.

A digger has big wheels or crawler tracks. It can go over bumpy ground.

There are different kinds of diggers. One kind of digger is called a backhoe.

Diggers move dirt.

They dig ditches.
They get the
ground ready
for buildings.

All done digging!

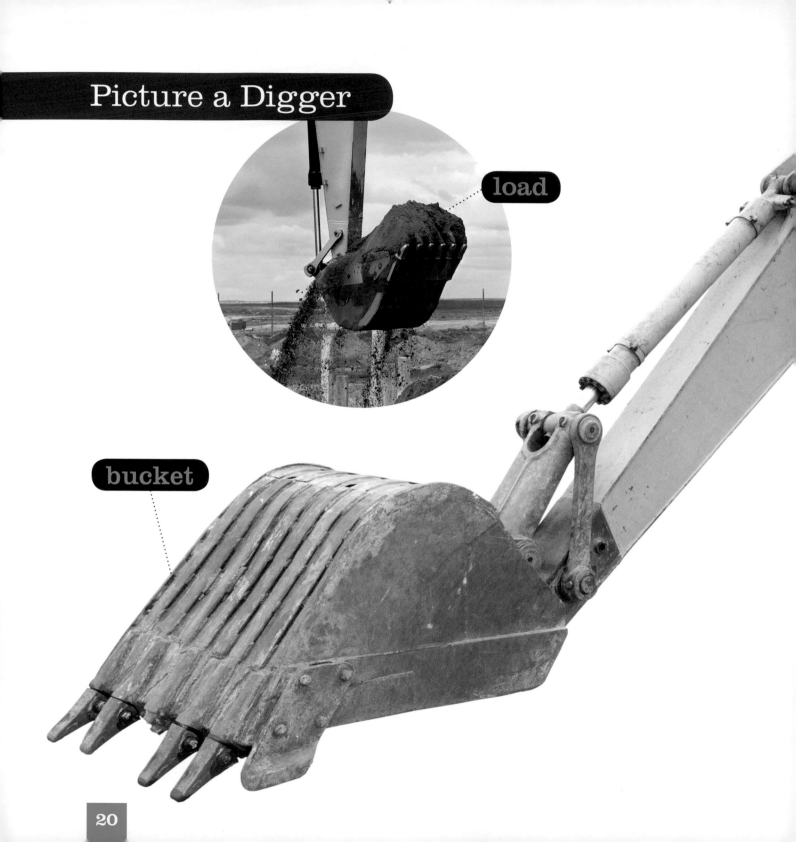

Picture a Digger

load

bucket

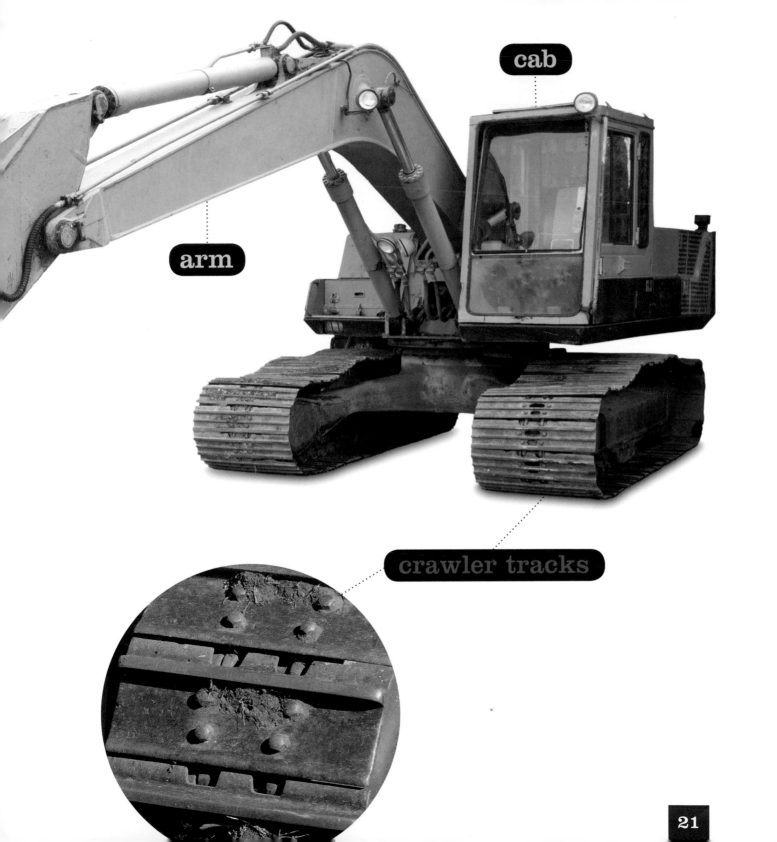

cab

arm

crawler tracks

21

Words to Know

arm: a long part that can reach and move

backhoe: a kind of digger that has two arms

crawler tracks: big, strong belts that go around like wheels

ditches: long, deep cuts in the ground

Read More

Gardner, Charlie, ed. *See How They Go: Diggers.*
New York: DK Publishing, 2009.

Sobel, June. *B Is for Bulldozer: A Construction ABC.*
San Diego: Gulliver Books, 2003.

Websites

Big Trucks for Kids
http://www.bigtrucksforkids.com/digger-truck-videos.html
This site has pictures and videos of diggers at work.

Free Construction Coloring Pages
http://www.squidoo.com/free-construction-coloring-pages
This site has digger pictures. You can print and color them.

Index